A Guide to Growing Tasty Vegetables

(From a Lifetime of Experience)

By

Robert Allen Morris

Orchid Springs Publishing, LLC
329 N. Park Ave., Floor 2
Winter Park, FL 32789

Table of Contents

Forward

Some of my fondest early memories are of working in my grandfather's vegetable garden with him when I was only about six or seven years old. My grandmother was a fantastic cook, and I remember her fresh, tasty vegetables: deep red juicy tomatoes, black-eyed peas cooked with home-smoked bacon, fried okra, and sweet corn dripping with melted butter. I remember early on a summer morning, the sun just beginning to shine its golden light over the trees, drops of silver dew glistening on blades of grass, the air filled with the songs of wrens, and mockingbirds, and the aroma of honeysuckle, going into the garden, cutting open a ripe watermelon while it was still on its vine, and eating the heart, the sweet juice dripping down my chin. The look of pride in my grandfather's eyes when at our Fourth of July picnic, all of our meal was provided by his labors – fried chicken from chickens he'd raised, vegetables from his garden, and that sweet watermelon. Everywhere I've lived for more than a couple of years, I've grown a vegetable garden – even when I was in college. When the chill of winter gives way to crisp spring mornings, and the air is filled with the perfume of blooming flowers and shrubs, I'm as excited as a kid on Christmas morning in anticipation of planting our spring garden. To me gardening is much more than just a way to produce vegetables. Its exercise, fresh air, sunshine, the joy of making and watching things grow, and the pride of producing tasty, nutritious food for your family and friends.

Working in My Vegetable Garden In Our Back Yard On Lake Ruby

Introduction

Note: **This guide is written based on my experiences in Florida. The main things that differ for other states are the planting dates, which can be obtained by contacting your local agricultural extension agent at the county agricultural extension office. In reality, a spring garden should not be planted until the risk of freezing temperatures is gone, and a fall garden should be planted so the vegetables can be harvested before freezing temperatures begin.**

Until only about 50 years ago, home vegetable gardens were as important a part of rural households as televisions and computers are today. But now they are rare, because modern agricultural production, marketing and distribution technologies have made the supermarket an equally economical source of vegetables as growing them in the family garden. And while maybe not quite as fresh or tasty, today's vegetables from the supermarket are of equal quality to home grown vegetables, and they are available year-around.

So why have a vegetable garden? For the same reasons some love golf, fishing, sailing, camping, hunting, etc. Because it can be fun and enjoyable. But like any other hobby, you won't know if you like it unless you try it. And you may find out that vegetable gardening is not for you, or that it's a passion for you.

Other than the time of year that they are grown, the main difference in spring and fall/winter gardens is the types of plants grown. Sweet corn, black-eye peas, lima beans, green beans, okra, squash, cucumbers, watermelons tomatoes, bell peppers, etc. are typical warm season vegetables for spring gardens, while collard, mustard and turnip greens, cabbage, lettuce, onions, carrots, broccoli, cauliflower, radish, etc. are typical cool season vegetables for fall/winter gardens. Potatoes, which are planted in January (in central Florida), fall in between but are considered a cool season vegetable. Many cool season vegetables will not grow well in temperatures above 75 degrees F. and prefer temperatures in the 60-70 degree F. range. In central and south Florida, many of the warm season vegetables, such as sweet corn, tomatoes, cucumbers, black-eye peas, lima beans and others, can also be grown in fall/winter gardens.

Planning

Planning a garden should begin at least three months before it will be planted, to give time for soil testing, adjusting soil pH (acidity) if needed, ordering quality seed, and land preparation. If you live where the ground is frozen from December to April, that means you should plan your garden and adjust the soil pH in the fall, before the ground freezes. The garden should be located in an open area that receives at least 6 hours of direct sunlight daily, and should receive both morning and afternoon sun. If you can't modify your lawn irrigation system to also serve your garden, or install an underground irrigation system with a well and pump, then be sure the garden is located close enough to spigots to enable watering with hoses and sprinklers.

Determine the types of vegetables you will grow. Consult your county's agricultural extension office and county agent to determine the types of vegetables that grow best in your area, the planting dates for spring and fall gardens, and the types of vegetables that grow best in spring versus fall gardens. Your county agent will have a college degree in agriculture and their job is to provide residents of that county with free advice about all aspects of gardening, farming and agriculture. They can be an extremely valuable resource for home gardeners.

On a sheet of paper, draw out the garden to scale and draw in each row and the spacing between rows, labeling the rows by type of vegetable to be planted. This ensures that adequate space is available for the different vegetables you plan to grow, and it also serves as a useful map on the day of planting. Sweet corn requires cross-pollination in order to produce good yields and ears completely filled out with kernels. Thus, at least three contiguous rows should be planted. If the garden layout is for long rows, three or four half or quarter rows next to each other is a better design for sweet corn rather than one or two long rows.

The tools needed consist of a short-tined garden rake; a hoe and tool file to keep it sharp; if you are going to plant potatoes, a potato rake; a push plow with a 5-tine cultivator, and also a furrow plow and moldboard plow, which you may or may not need; a 1 to 2 gallon insecticide sprayer; four tent stakes and nylon twine, first for staking off the garden area and later for marking the rows; a broad-cast type lawn fertilizer spreader; a four-foot section of 2X4 for packing dirt on top of seeds; and a wheel barrow or garden utility cart to carry and hold tolls, seed, fertilizers, etc. You will also need a rear-tined garden tiller for soil preparation, but since these can cost over a thousand dollars, its best to rent one for the first garden that you plant to be sure that this is a hobby that you like and will do on a regular basis.

The push plow can be purchased at many farm and garden stores. It has two plow handles and a large spoke wheel. Under the wheel is a place to attach various implements with a bolt and nut. Most push plows come with a small moldboard plow (it is a flat, odd-shaped steel blade), a pointed furrow plow, and a five-tined cultivator (shown on the push plow in this picture). If potatoes will be grown, a potato rake will be needed to harvest the potatoes. A potato rake is shaped like a hoe, but has 4 thick tines about 6-7 inches long in place of a hoe blade. If tomatoes are to be planted, some type of tomato stakes will be required, but more about this later. This booklet is not necessarily recommending the brands of the tools shown here. Other brands of tools may be as suitable or more suitable for these tasks. These brands were chosen because I am familiar with them.

Garden Push Plow, Courtesy of Earthway Products

5-Tine Cultivator,

Courtesy of Agri Supply

Furrow Plow, Courtesy of Lehman's

Moldboard Plow, Courtesy of Lehman's

Potato Rake, Courtesy of True Temper

Insecticide Sprayer, Courtesy of Northern Tool & Equipment

Fertilizer Spreader, Courtesy of Northern Tool & Equipment

Garden Tiller, Courtesy of Troy-Bilt

Courtesy of Troy-Bilt

Soil Preparation

After the garden's location is determined, mark the garden's boundaries by staking the area off with tent stakes and string. Next, collect soil samples for nutrient and acidity testing. While soil testing kits can be obtained at retail farm and garden stores, I've never found them satisfactory. A soil testing kit can be obtained from your county extension office with directions on how to use it. The technically correct approach is to test two composite soil samples, one for pH (acidity) and one for macronutrients (nitrogen, phosphorus and potassium). However, I don't usually do the test for macronutrients since I believe that using pre-mixed fertilizers gives just as good of results as mixing my own, and these required macronutrients can and will be adjusted at planting and during the growing process by simply using the correct fertilizer mix and quantity, but more will be explained about this in the section entitled "Fertilizing".

The test for pH is a very important test. The best pH range for most vegetable gardens is between 5.5 and 7.0, with 6-6.3 being ideal for most vegetables (except potatoes, where 5.5-6 is preferable). If soil pH is below 5.0 it is too acid and the result will be poor root development and poor performance of nitrogen-fixing bacteria, which will stunt or limit plant growth.

When we lived in Bradenton, Florida the soil in our garden plot was heavy flat woods soil. I decided to plant a garden "at the last minute" and did not do a soil test for pH. The result was best exemplified by the sweet corn. Rather than grow to its desired 6+ feet in height, the cornstalks only grew about two feet tall, and never made any corn. Subsequent testing showed a very acid soil, which I should have known the heavy flat woods soils would probably be. The tomatoes, which are fine in higher acid soils but still fine with less acid soils, did terrific.

For the composite soil sample (these directions will be in the kit) you will remove the sod and topsoil down about 3-4 inches deep from several sites representative of the garden area. Then with a trowel, dig about a half-cup of soil from each of the sample sites. Thoroughly mix the soil samples together to form a composite sample. Put (all or part of) the composite sample in the container provided and take it to the extension office. From there it will be taken to a lab for analysis. The results will probably take 1-2 weeks from when you deliver it to the extension office, and they will provide instructions on how to interpret the report.

If the soil pH is too low (below 5.0), increase it by applying lime at the rate recommended in the soil test evaluation you received from the extension office. This application of lime should ideally be about 2-4 months before the date the garden is to be planted, but after the soil has been prepared for planting. Although less than ideal, if adequate time was not allowed and the soil is too acid, lime can be applied as late as three weeks before planting if necessary. Just make sure the lime is thoroughly mixed into the soil to a depth of 6-8 inches and receives rainfall or irrigation water to promote the chemical reaction.

If the soil pH is too high (7.0 or higher), the result will be deficiencies of micronutrients such as manganese, iron, zinc and copper, which can reduce plant performance and crop yields. If your soil pH is naturally above 7.0, there is probably limestone, marl or shells present in your soil and there may be no way of permanently lowering your soil's pH. To offset the affects of this high pH, micronutrients can be added to, or purchased as part of, the fertilizers used. And sulfur can also be used to help reduce soil pH. This will be covered under the section entitled "Fertilizing".

The first step to soil preparation is to mow the garden spot. Then there are two approaches to preparing this "new land" for planting. If you live on a small farm or ranchette, probably the best method to prepare the soil for planting is to use a moldboard turn plow pulled by a tractor and turn under the vegetation and roots where it will decompose and add organic matter to the garden. Ideally this plowing should be done about 3-4 months before planting, to give the vegetation time to decompose. If the soil requires liming, broadcast the required lime over the plowed soil within a week or two of plowing and use a disk harrow pulled by a tractor to incorporate the lime into the soil. Then re-disc the soil the week before planting to make a seedbed. Although most readers will not live on farms and use a tractor to prepare the soil for their gardens, below are pictures of me plowing and disc harrowing a field when I was a teenager.

Most home gardeners today don't have access to a tractor, turn plows, and disc harrows, or if they did, they couldn't get them into their garden spots, so this second soil preparation method will be the one used by most home gardeners, me included. If your garden requires liming, the soil should be prepared 2-4 months before planting to give the lime time to adjust the soil pH. If your soil does not require liming, you can wait until about 3-4 weeks before planting to begin preparing the soil. If the chosen garden spot contains a lush turf grass such as floratam, or a very robust carpet of bahai grass, you may need to have someone cut and remove the sod. If it is simply a light carpet of bahia grass or mostly weeds, after the garden spot has been mowed to the height of a normal lawn, use a herbicide such as Round-up to kill all grass and weeds over the staked off garden area. This will probably take about two weeks after the herbicide is applied.

Plowing Land with a Moldboard Plow

Using a Disc Harow on Plowed Soil to Prepare A Seedbed

Once the grass and weeds are dead, the stakes and string marking the garden spot can be removed. Use the garden rake to rake and pull up all the dead grass and weeds along with their roots that you can. If the herbicide was applied correctly, this layer of grass, weeds and attached roots can fairly easily be "peeled" off the top of the ground. Pull the dead grass and roots to the ends and sides of the garden and haul them off or burn them. This raking of dead grass, weeds and their roots is important before initially tilling the soil, otherwise the tiller will simply mix all this material into the soil where it will reduce the quality of the seed bed. While this vegetative material could add useful organic matter to the garden, without a turn plow, I believe it's difficult to adequately incorporate it into the soil.

Obtain a motor-powered **rear-tined** garden tiller. I believe rear-tined tillers are the most powerful of the hand-operated tillers, and they are self-propelled. For first time gardeners, it's probably better to rent a tiller than to invest the $1,000- $3,000 to purchase one, to have the experience of your first garden so you can make an informed decision as to whether you like being a gardener on a regular basis enough to buy a tiller. Rear-tined tillers can be rented by the half-day or day from Home Depot, Lowes and many equipment rental stores. My favorite tillers are those made by Troy-Bilt and Honda. Rent the largest one they have.

It will probably require tilling the same area at least twice and maybe three times to get an adequate seed bed. After tilling the soil the first time, again take the garden rake and rake any remaining roots from grass and weeds that the tiller turned up to the sides of the garden, and haul them off as trash. Once the roots are raked out of the garden spot, if the soil requires liming, spread the lime and till the garden spot again to mix the lime into the soil. Unless the soil is frozen, the garden should then be tilled with the rear-tined tiller once every three weeks to control weeds until fertilized and planted. If the garden does not require liming, after raking any remaining roots out of the garden following the initial tilling, till it a second time to improve the seed bed.

One day to one week before planting, evenly broadcast the required fertilizer over the garden area. Then use the rear-tined tiller to till the area again and mix the fertilizer into the soil. If the garden did not require liming or cutting and removing the sod, you can probably till the garden, rake up any remaining roots, till the garden again to improve the seed bed, then fertilize the garden and till this into the soil a day or two before planting. Once the initial fertilizer application is tilled into the soil, the rear-tined garden tiller will not be needed until a new garden is planted.

Fertilizing

Most commercial fertilizers sold at retail farm and garden stores are pre-mixed fertilizers that contain the three key macronutrients that all plants require for growth: nitrogen (N), phosphorus (P), and potassium (K). This analysis is expressed on a tag located on the fertilizer bag. For example, an analysis of 10-3-9 means that this fertilizer contains 10% nitrogen by weight, 3% phosphorus, and 9% potassium. Thus, a 50-pound bag of this fertilizer would provide 5 pounds of nitrogen, 1.5 pounds of phosphorus and 4.5 pounds of potassium. The remainder of the weight of the bag is filler to facilitate even distribution of the macronutrients when the fertilizer is applied. These macronutrients, particularly nitrogen, are more likely to be deficient in the soil due to leaching than micronutrients like copper, magnesium, zinc, etc. In fact, nitrogen so readily leaches out of all but the most organic of soils, that testing labs evaluating macronutrients usually don't test for nitrogen, assuming it's always needed. Even though micronutrients such as copper, zinc and magnesium don't leach out of the soil as readily as nitrogen, it's still a good idea to use fertilizers that contain these micronutrients as well as the macronutrients nitrogen, phosphorus and potassium.

If a macronutrient evaluation was done from a composite soil sample, as was mentioned earlier, the soil test report will provide recommendations about the quantities of phosphorus and potassium that are required for your soil. For example, the report may recommend that in addition to 100 pounds of nitrogen per acre, your soil needs 70 pounds of phosphorus and 110 pounds of potassium per acre. The fertilizer analysis that is required is 10-7-11, or maybe 8-6-9 would be close enough to the actual 8 - 5.6 - 8.8 required. If you decide to do the macronutrient soil test, probably the most accurate way to get the ideal fertilizer for your soil is to purchase and apply the macronutrients separately or blend your own mix. Ammonium nitrate (33% nitrogen), ordinary superphosphate (20% phosphorus) and muriate of potash (60 % potassium), can be purchased as separate macronutrients that you can apply separately or blend to your required specifications. However you may have to special order them, and in 50 or 100 pound quantities, since most retail stores tend to carry pre-mixed blends rather than these separate macronutrients. Then you either need to apply them separately in three applications, or construct a blending apparatus and purchase filler to ensure an even and consistent mixing of these separate macronutrients. For example, you don't want one row in the garden to receive mostly nitrogen while another row receives mostly potassium.

These are reasons that I don't bother to do a soil test for macronutrient requirements in a home garden. For the typical Florida soils, and most types of vegetables grown in Florida, I believe a pre-mixed balanced fertilizer for the initial applications, such as 10-10-10 or 8-8-8 works just fine. These blends can be found in virtually all retail farm and garden stores, including Lowes and Home Depot. If this mix results in excessive phosphorus or potassium, it will not matter as long as guidelines for application rates don't exceed required nitrogen levels. And since nitrogen is usually the macronutrient that leaches out of soils the most and the soonest, it can be assumed to be almost totally missing in the soil. Thus, its requirement drives the fertilizer application rates and timing. Since there is assumed to be little or no nitrogen present, fertilize according to nitrogen requirements of the vegetables, and with a balanced fertilizer mix, phosphorus and potassium are also provided at the same levels. If the balanced fertilizer mix results in too little phosphorus or potassium (not likely, but possible) this will occur for some vegetables and not for others, since phosphorus and potassium requirements differ by type of vegetable. Inadequate amounts of these macronutrients can be detected by leaf color and plant performance and supplemented later for those vegetables that may need it, during plant growth. Check with your county extension agent for recommended macronutrient mixes for soils in your area.

If soil pH runs on the high side (7.0 or above), additional micronutrients will probably be needed beyond those that may be part of the pre-mixed blend of macronutrients you are using. They can be purchased separately as either micronutrient blends, usually copper, manganese, iron, zinc and magnesium in one micronutrient fertilizer mix or by type of micronutrient. Apply this according to recommendations from the soil test report and information on the package or container. Also, sulfur can be used to help lower soil pH. How much micronutrients and sulfur to use is part of the recommendations of the soil test report. For example one soil test I had done a number of years ago in another county recommended that I "apply one ounce of the micronutrient mixture (also recommended in the test report) per 100 square feet of garden space, and apply one pound of sulfur per 100 square feet of garden space".

For the sandy Polk County ridge soil that I live on, four fertilizer applications are usually best due to leaching caused by the sandy soil. The first application should ideally be 2-4 days before planting, but can be as long as one week or as short as one day before planting, and it should be evenly broadcast over the garden space. While fertilizer can be broadcast by hand, a lawn fertilizer broadcaster will ensure more even distribution, which is important. Broadcast .2-.3 pounds of nitrogen per 100 square feet of garden space. Thus, with a 10-10-10 fertilizer, which is 10% nitrogen, broadcast .2/.1 to .3/.1 or 2 to 3 pounds of the 10-10-10 fertilizer mix per 100 square feet of garden space. If your fertilizer is 8-8-8, it contains 8% nitrogen, so broadcast .2 /.08 to .3/.08, or 2.5 to 3.75 pounds of this fertilizer per 100 square feet of garden space. I use the upper end of this range for the sandy soil in my garden, and broadcast 3 pounds of 10-10-10 per 100 square feet. This broadcasted fertilizer should be tilled into the soil immediately after it is broadcasted, ideally using the rear-tined tiller, but the push plow with the five-tined cultivator attachment can also be used. When preparing soil for planting, it's best not to leave footprints because the compressed soil in the footprint promotes weed growth. Thus, if the rear-tined tiller is used to cultivate the fertilizer into the soil, walk to one side of it so no footprints are left behind it. If the push plow with the five-tined cultivator is used, rake the area smooth with a garden rake.

For planted or sowed seeds (not transplanted plants), the second fertilizer application should be done as granular fertilizer at planting. This application, like the remaining applications, is made in bands or strips along both sides of each row. Mark off the first row to be planted with stakes and string (see section entitled **"Planting"** for details about marking rows) and use the rake handle to make a small trench about an inch deep along the string where the row of seeds will be planted. The fertilizer should be applied in a band or strip about 2-3 inches on each side of the trench. The recommended application rate is .1 pound of nitrogen per 20 feet of row, which for a 10-10-10 fertilizer would be one pound of fertilizer per 20 feet of row, which should be applied as one-half pound per 20 feet of row on each side of the row.

There are two different ways that the fertilizer can be applied. One is to just apply it to the top of the soil 2-3 inches on each side of the trench where the seeds will be planted, then cultivate the fertilizer into the soil using the push plow with the 5-tined cultivator attachment and rake the cultivated area smooth. Another way is to use the furrow opener attachment on the push plow and make a furrow about two inches deep and 2-3 inches on each side of the trench where the seeds will be planted. Put the fertilizer into the furrow and cover it up by raking dirt over it from each side of the furrow.

I've had more success applying the fertilizer to the top of the soil than in a trench, probably because my sandy soil leaches so badly that by the time plants are large enough for roots to grow over to where the trenches with the fertilizer were, much of the fertilizer has leached away. Applying it to the top of the soil and plowing it in with the 5-tined cultivator, which spreads each band over about a 4-6 inch area, is really just like broadcasting it in a 9-12 inch wide area down the drill (seed row) where the seeds will be planted, so it's more readily available to the young plants. That is, as long as it's not concentrated directly in the trench where the seeds will be planted, otherwise it could burn the young plants. Finally, put the stakes and string back in place to mark the row (if you had to move them out of the way, I just leave them in place while fertilizing), remake the trench about 1-1.5 inches deep with the rake handle since some dirt will have fallen into the trench, and plant the seeds.

I find it easiest to apply fertilizer in bands using a large plastic cup. It will take some practice to get an even distribution, and not come up short before finishing a row, or have some left over. Often the wind and usually my aim require that the cup be held only about a foot above the ground to get the fertilizer band placed where it should be. To keep from getting a sore back from all this bending, I mounted a sturdy plastic cup (not the kind that comes in packages of 20, but rather the sturdy kind that soft drinks or beer is served in at sports events) on the end of a 3-foot long stick using two bolts, and nuts with washers to completely cover the holes drilled into

15

the bottom of the cup for attaching to the stick. Then I determined how much fertilizer was needed in the cup to band one side of a row by weighing the fertilizer, then putting it in the cup and marking the amount with a line using a black marking pen. I then simply fill the cup to this line with fertilizer, and with practice, I can get a pretty uniform band so my cup of fertilizer just runs out at the end of the row.

The third fertilizer application is also granular fertilizer and should be three weeks from planting, or about two weeks after the plants have emerged, and it should be done the same way, with the same type of fertilizer, in the same amounts. Bands of fertilizer should be about 3-4 inches to the side of the plants and applied to the top of the soil rather than in furrows as may have been done at planting. Cultivate the fertilizer into the soil using the push plow and the 5-tined cultivator attachment. Since this will also be a weed-control cultivation, finish by cultivating the balance of space between the rows of plants (the middles) and rake the cultivated area smooth.

Usually only one more fertilizer application is needed. This is called the side dressing, and it contains only nitrogen. The fertilizer used is ammonium nitrate, a granular fertilizer which is 33% nitrogen. This is applied 4-5 weeks after plant emergence, which is also 5-6 weeks after planting and 2-3 weeks from the third fertilizer application. This application of nitrogen provides the plants, which are now over half grown, with a substantial growth boost to "kick" them into robust growth and the development of their vegetables. This time from mid-growth cycle until crop development and maturity is also when the plants growth requirements are highest, and I believe these needs are best met with ammonium nitrate.

It will need to be ordered, since most retail garden stores do not carry it. But a 50-pound bag is less than $30, and if it is stored in an airtight container, it will last for a year supplying both the spring and fall garden. Ammonium nitrate can also be used on lawns, shrubs and citrus trees, with dramatic growth results. If you can't obtain ammonium nitrate, a substitute is a high-nitrogen, low or non- phosphorus fertilizer, such as 15-0-15. Phosphorus leaches out of the soil the least of the macronutrients so isn't needed in this fertilization since plenty is there from the earlier fertilizations. Potassium can always be used, although isn't nearly as important in this phase of plant growth as nitrogen.

Band ammonium nitrate the same as the previous fertilizer application, down both sides of each row, but now just even with the tips of the outside leaves of the plants. Apply one-fourth pound per 20 feet of row on each side of the row, which is a total of one-half pound per 20 feet of row. Cultivate it into the soil, cultivate the middles and rake the cultivated area smooth. If 15-0-15 is used, put it out at the same rate as the previous fertilization of 10-10-10, one pound per 20 feet of row, applied as one-half pound to each side of the row. This is the last fertilization that is required.

Tomatoes, green peppers, onions, broccoli, Brussels sprouts, cauliflower, lettuce and cabbage usually perform best if purchased as small plants, then transplanted into the garden. Do not band granular fertilizer along side the rows before planting transplants. Rather, when the plants are transplanted into the garden, water them with a liquid fertilizer such as Miracle-Gro or Grow More plant food mixed with water according to the instructions on the container. Miracle-Gro and Grow More are essentially very water-soluble mixed fertilizers. Miracle-Gro tomato plant food is 18-18-21, and 24-8-16 for the all-purpose, with micronutrients. Grow More is 15-20-25 for tomatoes and 15-15-15 or 20-20-20 for all-purpose, also with micronutrients. Water plants with the liquid fertilizer once each week until the third fertilizer application to the whole garden, which should be three weeks after the plants were transplanted (if they were transplanted when the rest of the garden was planted). From then on, follow the same granular fertilizer program for them as for the rest of the garden.

Fall/winter garden crops such as mustard, collard and turnip greens, and carrots, all work best planted as seeds since they are sowed rather than spaced a number of inches apart like broccoli, cauliflower and cabbage. Although granular fertilizer should be banded alongside the row as described earlier at planting, these plants are so small for the first few weeks after plant emergence that they should be fertilized with liquid all- purpose plant food weekly, beginning with one week after plant emergence until the plants are about 2 inches tall (usually about 4 weeks after planting). Then granular fertilizer can be banded about 2 inches to each side of the row at the same rate as for other vegetables, .1 pound of nitrogen per 20 feet of row. For 10-10-10, that's one pound of fertilizer per 20 feet of row, applied as ½ pound on each side per 20 feet of row. Side dress with ammonia nitrate 2-3 weeks after the last application of mixed fertilizer.

Potatoes also require a different fertilizer program. Nitrogen and potassium are the key nutrients required for optimum potato production. Rather than broadcast 10-10-10 or 8-8-8 fertilizer over the area where potatoes will be grown along with the rest of the garden, its better to broadcast a 10-4-7 or some mix that is mostly nitrogen and potassium, but has some phosphorus, evenly over the area that only the potatoes will be grown on. Since potatoes are essentially planted in Florida between the planting times of fall and spring gardens (late January), they are all that you will be planting at this time. In other states, they may be planted at the same time other vegetables are planted. Mark the area off where the potatoes will be planted, then anytime from a day to a week before planting, broadcast fertilizer at the rate of .15 pound of nitrogen, .06 pound of phosphorus and .105 pound of Potassium per 100 square feet. This would be .15/.1 = 1.5 pounds 10-4-7 fertilizer per 100 sq. ft.

Cultivate this into the soil using either a rear tined tiller or the push plow with the five-tined cultivator attachment and rake the area smooth with the garden rake. At plant emergence, apply these same rates per 20 ft. of row, but since the row now has plants, the fertilizer should be banded on both sides of the row. This would be .075 pound of nitrogen, .03 pound of phosphorus and .05 pound of potassium on each side of the row (.75 pounds 10-4-7 on each side per 20 feet of row). This fertilizer should be placed in a furrow and covered with dirt rather than on top of the soil and cultivated in. Use the furrow attachment for the push plow and make a furrow about 2 inches deep, 2-3 inches wide and 3-4 inches to each side of the row of plants and band the fertilizer in this furrow, then cover the furrow with dirt. Make another fertilizer application the same as this one but 4-6 inches to the side of the plants in three to four weeks. No other fertilization is needed for the potatoes.

For heavier, less sandy soils, not as much fertilizer or as many fertilizer applications will be needed because not as much fertilizer will be lost due to leaching. For these heavier soils, only three applications of fertilizer are required, one broadcast before planting, the second banded two weeks after planting, and the ammonia nitrate application 5-6 weeks after planting. The initial broadcast application should be at the rate of .3-.4 pounds of nitrogen per 100 square feet and skip the banded fertilization at planting. The second fertilizer application should be banded, and in the same way and at the same rates as the third fertilizer application on sandy ridge soils, but it should be two weeks after planting, which should be about one week after plant emergence. The rest of the fertilization program should be the same as for the sandy soils.

Planting

To obtain planting dates and types of vegetables best suited for your area, contact the county agricultural extension office for your county, as was recommended earlier under "Planning." For Central Florida, I believe a spring garden should be planted during the first or second week of March, with potatoes, tomatoes and okra being exceptions. Okra should be planted later than these dates, around the first week of April. Tomatoes should be planted earlier, around the first week of February and potatoes should be planted in late January. I believe cool season crops in a fall/winter garden should be planted around the first week of October and warm season crops like sweet corn, black-eye peas or tomatoes planted in a fall garden should be planted in mid-September. I believe that tomatoes in central Florida work best in a fall/winter garden because insects aren't as prevalent in January and February when the tomatoes will be harvested as they are in May, when the tomatoes will be harvested from a spring garden.

For a spring garden in central Florida, the objective is to plant early enough that the crops have been produced and harvested before the middle of June. That's because by June in Central Florida, the hot damp nights facilitate the growth of various funguses and insects also become much more prolific. Plants that still aren't old enough to produce their crops by June run a high risk of being negatively impacted by the central Florida climate, and if nothing else, yields will suffer. This is one key reason that commercial vegetable farms in Central and South Florida are pretty much finished for the season by June.

Okra is an exception to this summer weather problem. Okra plants often struggle in the cool nights of early March, which is why they should be planted in early April. But they thrive in the warm humid climate of Central Florida in June and July. I've never had a problem with okra succumbing to fungus or insect damage in the summer. It seems to be immune to everything, and it really grows well. Tomatoes, on the other hand, suffer most from this hot weather problem, which is the reason for the early planting dates for tomatoes. Tomatoes should be planted early enough that they are ready to begin harvesting by mid May. A fall/winter garden should be planted early enough to harvest before a freeze can damage the crop. Most seed and plant suppliers either do or can provide information about the days from planting to maturity for each of the vegetable seeds or plants they sell.

While retail garden stores sell seeds in paper packets, and some in bulk bins, I've had some bad experiences purchasing seeds from local stores. One year, the corn didn't come up within a week as it should have, so we bought more seeds from another place and replanted, but only a few of these seeds germinated. Then we bought seeds from still another store, but by this time we were so late planting that the corn yields were low. I think the best way to procure seeds is to order them from one of the seed catalogs. My favorite is Burpee. For plants to transplant, such as tomatoes and peppers, local retail garden stores are a fine source.

Use tent stakes and twine to mark each row before planting it, so that it's spaced correctly and straight. For example, if your rows are 36 feet long, tie about 38 feet of twine to two tent stakes. Then, using a yardstick, measure about a foot outward from the edge of the garden at the end of the row, and drive the stake into the ground in this spot. Then do the same at the other end of the row. Thus, measure out a foot from the edge of the garden on each end of the row. Then push a tent stake in the ground at that spot on each end of the row, stretching the twine attached to the tent stakes tightly, marking the row. Then again, if you have 36-inch wide rows here, measure over 36 inches from these tent stakes and, using the second set of tent stakes to which you should attach 38 feet of twine, mark this second row. While not required, I like to mark the rows two at a time this way, because it helps me keep the upcoming row and it's spacing in perspective.

Since most vegetable seed should be planted only 1 to 1 ½ inches deep, I make the furrow to plant them into with a rake or hoe handle rather than using a furrow attachment on the push plow, which tends to make a furrow that's too deep. Take the hoe or the rake, and using the top of the handle, make a trench about 1-2 inches deep along side the tightly stretched string on the first marked row. Put the seed in the trench at the spacing indicated in **Tables 1 and 2.** Then, using the garden rake, cover the seed with the right amount of dirt to put the seed at the depth shown in **Tables 1 and 2,** making sure it's not covered too deeply. This will probably leave much of the trench made to plant the seeds intact, thus the seeds will be in the bottom of a trench with about one inch sides, which is okay. Cover the seed by pulling soil over it with a garden rake. After the seed is covered, use a 3-4 foot long 2X4 to **lightly** pack the dirt on top of the seeds by laying it into the trench on top of the soil covering the seeds. Lightly packing the dirt over the seeds in this manner helps seal moisture around the seed, to improve germination. Commercial planters have a "press wheel" that follows behind the mechanical planter to pack the dirt over the seeds.

If your garden spot is prone to have standing water after a rain, and can't be drained well enough to prevent standing water for more than 12 hours, you may need to make beds to plant in to insure that excess water in the root zone is drained. The easiest way is to use a turn plow on a tractor and throw dirt from right to left, then turn the tractor around and come down the other side, throwing another furrow of dirt from left to right, so the plowed dirt from the two furrows is thrown together into a bed about 6-8 inches high. A much shallower bed (3-4 inches high) can be made with the turn plow attachment on the push plow. Or you can make beds by hand using a hoe and rake. I generally don't like to have gardens in such poorly drained soils, because the cultivation necessary to control weeds often partially flattens the beds, and even with beds, that rare torrential downpour will likely still drown some of the garden.

The planting densities for seed in **Tables 1 and 2** are greater than the spacing for the plants. That's because it's not uncommon to have less than 100% germination of the seed. For example, if you get 75% germination on sweet corn, spacing the seed three inches apart insures you can thin the tiny corn plants to one plant every 12 inches and not have skipped areas the way you would if you had planted the seed 12 inches apart. Thinning of the newly emerging plants should be when they are only 2-3 inches tall, which is usually only about a week from when they emerge. This gives enough time to insure the ones not thinned are going to do okay. Waiting longer until the plants are larger runs the risk of disturbing the delicate root zones of plants not thinned when the plants next to them are pulled up.

Once the seeds are planted, water the garden with about ¼ inch of water every night for the first week to help improve germination and keep the soil moist around the newly emerging plants. You will need a rain gauge or gauges to determine how much water you are putting on the garden. Most farm and garden stores sell them. They can be mounted on a post, or some have a stake bottom that enables sticking them in the ground. The watering needs to be in the very late afternoon or night so the seeds stay in moist ground for about 10 hours before the sun comes up and dries out the thin layer of soil covering them. If it rains, use your rain gauge to determine how much water your garden received. If it was less than ¼ inch, water them that night. If it was ¼ inch or more, do not water them the day/night it rained. If it was an inch or more, do not water them for 2-3 nights after it rained, depending on how wet the soil remains.

Planted seeds should emerge 6-10 days after they were planted. If they still haven't emerged two weeks from when they were planted, they should be replanted. Use the push plow with the 5-tine attachment to cultivate over the area where the seeds were planted. Also cultivate the rest of the area around that row including the middles. Rake the area smooth and replant. There is no need to re-fertilize unless getting a torrential rain with several inches of water that drowned the newly emerging seeds was the reason they didn't come up. However, you will need to fertilize a week from when these newly planted seeds emerge since it will have been about four weeks since the original planting when this area was fertilized. Apply the fertilizer with bands down each side of the row of plants the same way that growing plants are normally fertilized. For this row, the fertilizer schedule, including laying by after applying ammonium nitrate, will now be later by the amount of time it took to replant than for the rest of the garden.

Tomatoes, bell peppers, onions, broccoli, Brussels sprouts, cauliflower, lettuce and cabbage should be transplanted into the garden from plants that are either grown from seeds in a planter box or purchased at a garden store. They should not be started as seed in the garden because they won't grow well. Nowadays, retail garden stores produce high quality plants, and it's easiest just to buy them there for the plants they carry that you want to grow. Once you bring the plants home, water them daily until you plant them, which should be within a few days of when they are purchased.

Stretch the twine to mark each row the same as in planting seeds. Mark each spot for a plant with a trowel, following spacing recommendations from **Table 1.** Dig a hole that enables putting the plant deep enough to cover it up to its bottom branches. Pour a liquid fertilizer in the hole, making sure it has been mixed to the correct strength with water according to the instructions. Put the plant in the hole (which should have liquid in it) and push the dirt tightly around it. Make a small ring of dirt around the plant so that when it's watered, the water stays at the base of the plant long enough to soak in rather than run off. Then water the newly planted plant again with the liquid fertilizer, also covering the leaves with this liquid.

If the transplanted plants are part of a garden with newly planted seeds, the nightly watering of the entire garden with ¼ inch of water for the first week after planting will also meet the watering needs of the transplanted plants as well. If there are only tomato and pepper plants, they should be watered daily for the first week, and in the late afternoon or night. Watering them at mid-day or early afternoon runs the risk that the water and the hot sunshine will scald them.

Staked tomato plants, as their name suggests, must be staked. Once the plants are about two feet tall, the increasingly prolific branches will need to be tied to something to support them or the whole plant will end up on the ground and rot. I have never been able to buy tomato stakes that are sturdy or tall enough to support my tomatoes. If planted and fertilized according to the recommendations in this paper, your tomato plants should grow about 5-6 feet tall, and each put on 40 or more tomatoes. That ultimately requires sturdy support. My solution is to build a wooden fence close enough to the tomato plants that they can be tied to the fence. I set 8 ft. long landscape posts, which can be purchased for only about $3.00 each, about 2 feet deep and 8 feet apart. Then I nail 2X4's to the posts, spacing them about two feet apart, with the first 2X4 about 2 feet from the ground. When the tomato plants grow enough that their branches begin to sag, the branches should be tied to the 2x4's on this "fence" so that no branch is allowed to touch or get near the ground, where moisture and unwelcome organisms flourish. Use large cotton twine for tying branches. Thin nylon twine is more than sturdy enough, but once the tomatoes begin to grow and add weight to the branches, this thin twine cuts into the soft green branches and damages them.

Potatoes purchased from a grocery store should not be planted in a home garden, they will not do well. Certified disease-free seed potatoes should be purchased from a retail garden store. Potatoes have buds known as eyes on the skin surface from which new plants sprout and grow. Seed potatoes should be cut so that each piece is about the size of an egg, with at least one eye per seed piece. The cut seed pieces should heal over before planting, which means they should be stored in a cool (60-65 degrees F.), dark, well-ventilated, humid place for one or two days before planting. Plant seed pieces about 4 inches deep and 3 inches apart. Water nightly with about ¼ inch of water until plant emergence. Sprouts should emerge about 10-14 days from planting. Several days after the plants emerge, thin to one plant every 6-8 inches and proceed with hilling.

Hilling is the act of adding soil to the top of the potato row. Since the seed piece was only planted 4 inches below the soil surface, there is the possibility that new potatoes will push up above the soil surface. These exposed tubers turn green in the sun and will be inedible. To prevent this, add 2-3 inches of additional soil on top of the potato row when the sprout first emerges from the soil. This soil can be obtained from the middles between the rows.

Carrots, mustard, turnip, and collard greens, radish, and other winter vegetables all have very tiny seeds that should only be planted only about ¼ - ½ inch deep. These tiny seeds are difficult to evenly distribute and not plant too deeply, particularly if soil is crusty. Instead of covering with soil from the garden, cover them with manufactured potting soil that has a very fine texture. Another method is to plant in a trench about 1 inch deep, but instead of covering them with soil, water them with overhead sprinklers, which will wash a light covering of soil over them from the sides of the trench they are planted in. Because they are planted so shallow, they should be planted in the late afternoon after the sun has gone down, and watered within an hour of planting. When plants from the sowed seeds emerge and grow about 2-3 inches tall, thin according to directions on the seed packet or in **Table 2.**

Irrigation

I believe overhead sprinkler irrigation is ideal for a vegetable garden because it simulates rainfall and it's the most effective way to evenly reach a diversity of plants of various heights. Also, with overhead irrigation there are no above-ground hoses to get in the way of cultivation activities the way there are with drip or micro-jet systems. The above ground pipes holding the sprinkler heads should be about 6 feet tall, otherwise, plants that grow tall such as corn, okra, and staked tomatoes may block the even distribution of the water. Sprinkler heads should be of the type that distributes water evenly in a circle about 12-15 feet in diameter. For our garden, we were able to get the company that installed our lawn irrigation system to install 9 evenly spaced irrigation sprinklers in our garden space that simply tied into our lawn system. The pipes are about 6 feet tall, and each have a sprinkler head that evenly sprays water in a 15 foot diameter circle. We can run this "watering zone" along with the lawn system or separately.

While this is ideal, a garden can also be watered with a hose and lawn sprinkler. However, depending on the size of the garden and number of separate hoses you can use, this may require moving the sprinklers around every hour or so to cover the garden. And you may need to erect strategically located posts on which to temporarily attach the sprinklers and hoses, in order for the distribution of water not to be blocked by plants. I have used hoses and lawn sprinklers quite effectively for a number of vegetable gardens.

As indicated under the section on planting, the garden should be watered nightly with ¼ inch of water, (about 15 minutes with my irrigation system) for the first week after planting. After that, water 2-3 times weekly with about one inch of water each time, unless there is rainfall. This 2-3 inches of water weekly includes rainfall, thus, you will need to rely on your rain gauge(s) to irrigate properly. I have one in the center of the garden and another on the edge, because sometimes due to wind, my sprinkler system is not perfect in its distribution of water. The rain gauges will show how much water has been put on the garden and will help determine how much to irrigate when there is also rainfall.

Two to three irrigations a week of about an inch each is a better irrigation program than watering nightly with less water. While the nightly watering with about ¼ inch of water was helpful in germinating the seeds, watering frequently with small amounts of water tends not to enable the water to soak deeply enough into the soil. The result is that the root systems of the growing plants form too shallow and wide since that's where the wet soil is. Soon cultivation activities to control weeds will also be shearing some of the roots of the vegetable plants. With 2-3 irrigations a week of about an inch of water each, between irrigations the plants will grow their roots downward toward the moist soil, which makes healthier plants. Also, look at the plants. If they are wilting by mid or late afternoon, more frequent watering, say every other day, may be needed. But don't water too much, or the fertilizer will leach out of the soil and be lost.

Once in response to plants that were withering by late afternoon, I put two inches of water on the garden. We then proceeded to get six inches of rainfall over the next 24 hours, and within a week, plants were growing pale in color. I had to re-fertilize the garden. If your garden gets more than three inches of rainfall at any one time, or more that six inches in any three day period and its been at least a week since your last fertilization, depending on how sandy and well drained your soil is, you may need to repeat the most recent fertilizer application due to leaching. Also, use of weather forecasts, which are more accurate now than they were 25 years ago, can prevent watering a garden the day before it rains.

Many gardening books suggest watering around dawn, pointing out that watering in late afternoon or at night keeps plants wet all night when there is no sunlight to dry them, which promotes fungus and insect damage. I think young vegetable plants respond best if they are watered at dusk, because they have moist/wet soil all night that is not dried out by the sun. However, for larger, more mature leafy plants such as melons, squash, and green beans, it's probably best to water around dawn, because the covering effect of the leaves when wet all night does promote fungus and mildew underneath the leaves. The time that the garden should not be watered is during the hottest part of the day. That wastes water due to evaporation and can scald the plants.

Weed Control

There are various herbicides that can be used for effectively controlling weeds, and a good herbicide program is critical to the economic success of today's commercial farming operations. However, I don't use chemical weed control in my vegetable garden. One of the reasons I have a garden is to work in it, and to benefit from the exercise. Thus, I control weeds the old fashioned way. By cultivating (with a push plow), and using a hoe to supplement the push plow if necessary.

Use the five-tined cultivator to cultivate the garden weekly from the week after it's planted until it is side dressed with ammonium nitrate. Obviously some of the required cultivations will follow required fertilizations. After every time the garden is cultivated, rake the cultivated area smooth with a garden rake, being careful to "rake out" footprints. Footprints compact the soil and improve the conditions for weed germination. For standard 36-inch wide rows, it usually takes four passes with the cultivator. One close to each of the two rows of plants, and two passes to adequately plow the middle between the two rows of plants. During the first couple of times, care must be taken not to cover the small plants with dirt. However, once the plants are larger, by about the third week, the cultivator can be used so that it throws dirt into the area between the plants in the plant row (the drill) and covers the emerging weeds that will be growing there as well.

Be careful as the plants get larger not to plow so close to the plants that their roots are damaged. Once most plants are about 5-6 weeks old and the ammonium nitrate has been applied, do not cultivate anymore. Continued cultivation beyond this time will do more harm than good, by damaging the large plants' roots that will begin growing into the middles. By this time, the vegetable plants will have such a head start on the weeds that the weeds that do grow will do minimum damage, and ultimately the larger vegetable plants will reduce weed growth by shading them. Exceptions to this are for onions, bell peppers, turnip greens, carrots and other vegetables with smaller plants that never get large enough to shade out weeds and whose roots don't spread out like those of sweet corn, okra, etc.

Potatoes should be "laid by" about 6 weeks after they were planted. This process entails throwing dirt into the drill, covering weeds that may be growing between the plants and more importantly, re-hilling to prevent growing potatoes from being exposed to the sun. While some dirt will have been thrown into the drill with the five-tined cultivator attachment, this requires more dirt, about 2 inches. It is usually easiest to do this with the turn plow attachment on the push plow, but it can also be done with a hoe.

Disease Control

Root and stem rots, wilts, mildews, rusts, bacterial spots, etc. can all be troublesome in Florida's hot humid climate. Sometimes they can't be controlled and plants will be lost. I've had squash, watermelons and green beans all succumb to diseases. The best cure is prevention. Scout the garden frequently looking for symptoms on leaves such as discoloration, a white film, yellowing, etc. Remove first diseased leaves to slow the spread. Describe the problem to someone who is knowledgeable at your garden store and ask which of their products they recommend to deal with it. Many common diseases can be controlled with either chlorathalonil, maneb, or mancozeb fungicide. Powdery mildews can be controlled with triadimefon, sulfur or benomyl and rusts with sulfur or ziram. Control bacterial spots with copper sulfate plus maneb or mancozeb. Sprays are more effective than dusts. Use the one gallon sprayer in the list of materials described at the beginning of this paper. Begin control efforts early and follow directions on product labels.

Insect Control

The list of insects that attack Florida vegetable gardens seems endless. Aphids, budworms, earworms, leaf minor, fleabeetles, spider mites, squash vineborers, thrips, whiteflys, cutworms, and mole crickets, to name only a few. And there are numerous pesticides to control these insects. But I don't use any of them. Having worked for one of the largest commercial vegetable producers in the U.S. (Duda), with over 30,000 acres of vegetable farms in Florida, California and Texas, I understand the importance of pesticides to the economic success of commercial vegetable farming. But I prefer not to deal with the mixing, clean-ups, precautions, etc. of most effective chemical pesticides. My only insect control is growing healthy, robust plants.

The planting dates, fertilizer and weed control practices covered here should enable producing such vigorous, fast-growing plants, that affects of insect damage will be minor. Tomatoes may be an exception to this, but in spite of high culls, I still get more than enough tomatoes from only 20 plants. If you decide to use chemicals to control insects and pests, contact your county agricultural extension office for advice.

Harvesting and Post-Harvest Handling

Once a crop begins to set on the vegetable plants, check frequently to see when it's time to harvest. Obviously tomatoes will be red,[1] bell peppers, green beans, and cucumbers will be fully formed, squash will be fully formed and yellow, etc. For peas and lima beans, pick several and shell them to see when they are ready. Watermelons are ready when they are fully formed and the stem turns brown. Okra is ready to pick when the pods are 3-4 inches long, and shouldn't be allowed to get much larger or they will be "woody" and tough.

Sweet corn will have a thick, fully formed ear, and the silk on the end of the ear will be dark brown and dry. To be sure, pick a typical ear, completely shuck it, and examine the entire ear. The cob should be well-filled with plump kernels that are not dented (dented kernels are a sign that it's over ripe and loosing moisture). Taste it raw, and it should taste sweet. The taste of sweet corn is affected by temperature and time more than any other vegetable. Although today's new varieties maintain their sugar levels longer than older varieties, the sugar content in corn still converts to starch fairly soon at room temperatures. Therefore, corn should be cooked, refrigerated or frozen within a few hours of picking. If refrigerated, it should be kept as cold as possible without freezing, ideally at 33-40 degrees F. and consumed within 3-4 days.

As a separate note, it absolutely amazes me that so many people don't have a clue how to select sweet corn when it's in the shuck at the supermarket. They partially shuck the ear to look at it, examine only about the first few inches of the ear near the silk end, where it's usual to find immature or damaged kernels even on sweet, well formed ears. Then they put the partially shucked ear back into the bin. This ruins that ear because it will now dry out and warm up faster, thus the sugar will turn to starch faster. And because it ruins perfectly good ears of corn, it raises the price that supermarkets have to charge for corn sold in the shuck. Corn sold in the shuck is not any better than shucked corn, but it's usually less expensive (even with the damage done by ignorant customers) and it is ideal for grilling and barbecues.

Growers do not harvest corn until its ready, and any immature or damaged ears are removed at the packinghouse, so most corn sold at the supermarket is good. If anything is wrong with the corn it's probably starchy and not sweet, which is caused by not chilling it quickly enough after harvest (it should be cooled to 35 degrees F. within an hour of harvest), by not keeping it cold enough during distribution (it should be kept at 33-35 degrees F. until displayed for sale) or letting it get too old. At 40 - 45 degrees, which is approximately the temperature of

---

[1] Tomatoes in Central and South Florida are usually best harvested when they are not fully ripe and greenish red in color. Fully ripe tomatoes in Florida are insect magnets so it's best to let them finish ripening on your porch or inside the house.

most refrigerated retail display cabinets, the shelf life of tasty sweet corn is 3-5 days, and at room temperature, which is what most corn in the shuck is displayed at, its 2 days or less. But this can't be determined without tasting the corn.

Although you can't tell if temperature abuse has reduced the sweetness of corn without tasting it, the best way to select corn in the shuck at the supermarket is to select ears where the shucks haven't dried out and the silk is brown, then feel each ear that you buy to make sure that it is thick and well-formed. Beyond these observations, which are best made with the corn still in its shuck, shucking or partially shucking it will tell you nothing about its quality.

While sweet corn is all harvested either at the same time, or within a week, most vegetables will have multiple harvests. Tomatoes, bell peppers, squash, green beans, lima beans, peas, cucumbers, etc. will need to be harvested two or more times each week for several weeks. Okra is even more prolific. After the first few harvests, which may be several days apart because the plants are still smaller, okra can usually be harvested every other day for about two months.

Most potatoes are ready for harvest between 85-110 days after planting. For those potatoes that will not be stored, test their size by carefully digging below the potato plants with a potato rake and lifting the potatoes out of the soil. When a high percentage of these are large enough, they are ready to harvest. It requires special facilities to cure potatoes for long-term storage, but if kept in a cool, dark place they can be stored about 4 - 6 weeks in the home. Another way to improve storage life is to refrigerate them to 40-45 degrees F. If the potatoes will be stored after harvest, the plant should be allowed to die (mature) before harvest. Harvest the potatoes about 2-3 weeks after the plant has died. If a plant has not begun the maturation stage on its own, but digging shows that the potatoes are large enough, maturation can be induced by killing the tops of the plant. This can be done by cutting the plants off at the soil surface with shears or a knife. Leave the potato for about 2-3 weeks before digging them up so the tubers can mature. This mature tuber will store much longer than an immature tuber.

I usually sow mustard, collard and turnip greens when planting them. Harvest begins when they have leaves large enough to eat. The harvest is an on-going thinning, providing greens frequently over about a two month period and letting the remaining greens get larger.

The commercial packing, handling and distribution of vegetables sold in the supermarket requires time, while vegetables from the home garden can be consumed the same day or within a few days of harvest. Thus, the reason that vegetables from a home garden are usually tastier than those from the supermarket is because they are fresher. This is particularly true for sweet corn and okra. While modern plant breeding has created corn varieties that delay the turning of sugar to starch much longer than was true even 20 years ago, corn still drops in sugar content each day after it is harvested, particularly if it's not kept cold enough during distribution. Okra pods begin to loose some of their crispness on the second or third day after harvest.

There are numerous books that describe canning and freezing better than I can, so that will not be covered in this paper. The only vegetables I store are sweet corn, potatoes and tomatoes. The potatoes can be stored at room temperature in a well-ventilated cabinet. For corn and tomatoes, I simply wash them (I also shuck the sweet corn before freezing it), put them in plastic freezer bags and freeze them. The frozen tomatoes when thawed will turn to mush, which is good for soups and stews, and tastier than the stewed tomatoes from the supermarket. And because I freeze the sweet corn within an hour of picking it, it will be sweeter when boiled even than fresh corn from the supermarket. For all of the other vegetables I produce, we either consume them within a few days of harvest or give them to friends so they can also enjoy tasty fresh vegetables.

I hope this booklet is helpful to those who want to produce their own vegetables. Good luck and have fun!

Table 1. Vegetable Planting Information for Spring Gardens

Vegetable	Planting Depth in inches	Spacing in Inches Rows	Seeds	Plants	Yield Per 20 Ft. of Row	Days Until Harvest
Green Beans	1 to 2	36	2	2	10 lbs.	50-60
Lima Beans	1 to 2	36	2	4[a]	12 lbs. unshelled	65-75
Sweet Corn	1 to 2	36	4	12[a]	1 to 2 ears/stalk	60-95
Cucumbers	½	48	[b]	[b]	20 lbs.	50-65
Okra	1/2 to 1	36	4	12[a]	20 lbs.	50-75
Black-eyed Peas	1 to 2	48	2	2	18 lbs. shelled	60-90
Bell Peppers	Transplant Plants	36	NA	12	5 to 7 / plant	80-100
Yellow Squash	1	48	[c]	[c]	30 lbs.	40-55
Staked Tomatoes	Transplant plants	36	NA	24	20 per plant[d]	90-110
Watermelon	1 to 2	72	[e]	[e]	80 lbs.	85-95
Eggplant	Transplant Plants	36	NA	24	40 lbs.	90-110

[a] Plant seeds at the spacing for seeds and thin to the spacing for plants. This insures a good stand if some seeds do not germinate.

[b] Sow seeds over a mound 4 inches tall and 2 feet across. When plants are 2 inches tall, thin to 3 plants per hill. Hills should be 4 feet apart and rows 4 feet apart.

[c] Sow 5 seeds each 1 inch apart in row. Space these seed groups of 5 seeds each three feet apart. Rows should be 4 feet apart.

[d] Tomato plants will produce much more than this, but this is the yield after culling tomatoes with insect or bird damage.

[e] Sow 6 seeds over a hill 4 inches tall and 2 feet across. When plants are 3 inches tall, thin to 3 plants per hill. Hills should be 5 feet apart and rows 6 feet apart.

Source: Stevens, et. al. 1994

Table 2. Vegetable Planting Information for Fall Gardens

Vegetable	Planting Depth in inches	Spacing in Inches Rows	Seeds	Plants	Yield Per 20 Ft. of Row	Days Until Harvest
Broccoli[a]	Transplant	30	3[b]	15	10 lbs.	75-90
Cabbage[a]	Transplant	30	6[b]	18	25 lbs.	90-110
Carrots	¼	30	Sow	1[b]	20 lbs.	65-80
Cauliflower[a]	Transplant	30	5[b]	20	16 lbs.	70-90
Collard Greens	¼ to ½	30	Sow	2 to 5[c]	35 lbs.	70-80
Lettuce[a]	Transplant	30	3[b]	8	15 lbs.	50-90
Mustard Greens	¼ to ½	30	Sow	2 to 5[c]	25 lbs.	40-60
Onions Bulbing	Transplant	30	NA	6	20 lbs.	120-160
Potatoes©	4	42	3[b]	6 to 8	40 lbs.	85-110
Radishes	¼	30	1	1	8 lbs.	20-30
Staked Tomatoes[a]	Transplant	36	NA	24	20 per plant[d]	90-110
Turnip Greens	¼ to ½	30	Sow	4 to 6[c]	35 lbs.	40-60

[a] Transplanting plants will give a better crop

[b] Plant seeds at the spacing for seeds and thin to the spacing for plants. This insures a good stand if some seeds do not germinate.

[c] Collard, mustard and turnip greens should be thinned periodically as the plants grow. The thinned leaves can be consumed. While the original small plants will end up at the spacing shown in Table 2, there should not be a visible space between the plants until they are mature and harvest begins. Harvest will usually be spaced over several weeks and the fresh greens eaten as harvested.

[d] Tomato plants will produce much more than this, but this is the yield after culling tomatoes with insect or bird damage.

Source: Stevens, et. al. 1994

Table 3. Planting Dates for Central Florida

Spring Gardens

All vegetables but okra and tomatoes: February 15 – March 31

Tomatoes: February 1-15

Okra: April 1-15

Fall Gardens

All vegetables but potatoes: October 1 – October 31

Potatoes: Jan 21-31

_____

Note: Consult your local agricultural extension office to obtain the planting dates for
your area.

References

1. Boyette, M.D., L.G. Wilson and E.A. Estes. **Post Harvest Cooling and Handling of Sweet Corn.** North Carolina Cooperative Extension Service. December 1994.
2. Hochmuth, George and Edward A. Hanlon. **IFAS Standardized Fertilizer Recommendations for Vegetable Crops.** University Of Florida, Institute of Food and Agricultural Sciences. Revised, 1995.
3. Kidder, Gerald. **Lime and Liming – A Florida Perspective.** University of Florida, Institute of Food and Agricultural Sciences. March 1989.
4. Kidder, G. and J.M. Stephens. **Notes in Soil Science.** University of Florida, Institute of Food and Agricultural Sciences. April 1981.
5. Knott, James Edward. **Vegetable Growing.** Fifth Edition, Lea and Febiger, Philadelphia. January 1958.
6. Kucharek, Tom and Bob Dunn. **Diagnosis and Control of Plant Diseases and Nematodes in a Home Vegetable Garden.** University of Florida, Institute of Food and Agricultural Sciences. March 1994.
7. Pack, Jeffery, James White, and Chad Hutchinson. **Growing Potatoes in the Florida Home Garden.** University of Florida, Institute of Food and Agricultural Sciences. July 2003.
8. Simmone, E.H., Hochmuth, G.J., Maynard, D.N., Vavrina, C.S., Stall, W.M. Kucharek, T.A. and S.E. Webb. **Okra Production In Florida.** University of Florida, Institute of Food and Agricultural Sciences. September 2004.
9. Stephens, James M. **Tomatoes In The Florida Garden.** University of Florida, Institute of Food and Agricultural Sciences. April 1994.
10. Stephens, James M., R.A. Dunn, G. Kidder, D. Short and G.W. Simone. **Florida Vegetable Gardening Guide.** University of Florida, Institute of Food and Agricultural Sciences. Revised March 1994.

Also By Robert Allen Morris

Available at www.amazon.com in paperback or on Kindle

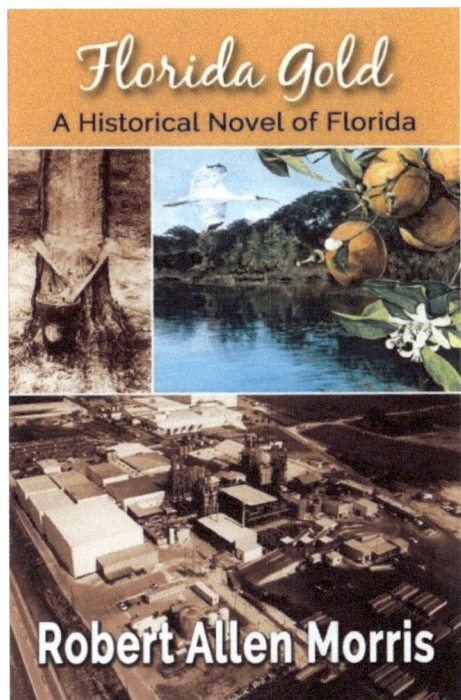

It's 1988, and Jack Thomas, the 73-year-old CEO of Tropical Juices, finally about to retire, reflects upon his life. The story quickly shifts back to Jack's birth in 1915 in a turpentine-making camp in rural Florida. The child of 15-year-old Irma Sue, who had been seduced by the son of a local moonshiner, Jack is to be raised as her brother by her parents, Pete and Margaret. Pete, however, is soon killed in a horse-riding accident. Irma Sue and Margaret move to Mobile, Alabama, hoping to earn enough money to bring Jack, left behind with friends, into a new home. Fortune smiles upon the attractive women, both marrying advantageously. The family reunites briefly before Jack is snatched to work the fields at one of Florida's illegal child labor camps. With the assistance of local Native Americans, Jack escapes from the camp as a teenager. He returns to Mobile, learns of further family catastrophe, then helps the feds bust up the camps. With seed money from a surprising source, Jack starts an orange-juice business in Florida, serves with distinction in World War II and continually expands his enterprise. By novel's end, he heads a multibillion-dollar company, although still more family losses make success bittersweet. Morris, an agricultural economist with over 30 years of experience in the citrus industry, brings plenty of insider knowledge and passion to this fictional work, managing to make sequences featuring the main character, Jack Thomas' savvy with concentrate, cartons that don't leak, and other innovations quite engaging. His narrative gets a bit overripe at times, given the seemingly never-ending and near-superhuman heroics of his main character as well as a rather melodramatic string of family tragedies. Still, this novel is ultimately highly entertaining, and a surprisingly juicy account about a key segment of commerce in the Sunshine State. --- *Kirkus Reviews*

Reviewed by Anne-Marie Reynolds for Readers' Favorite

Florida Gold by Robert Allen Morris was one of those 'wow factor' books. An amazingly told story, with real feeling put into the words. It's an unforgettable story, one that I could read over again and still take something new away from it. The characters are real and fit the story, the plot was well thought out and researched, and the whole book flows properly. Robert Morris is clearly a natural born storyteller and I would love to read more from him. – *Readers' Favorite*

Florida Gold was inducted into the Florida Citrus Archives on September 24, 2014. The event was hosted by the Lawton Chiles Center for Florida History on the Campus of Florida Southern College in Lakeland, Florida.

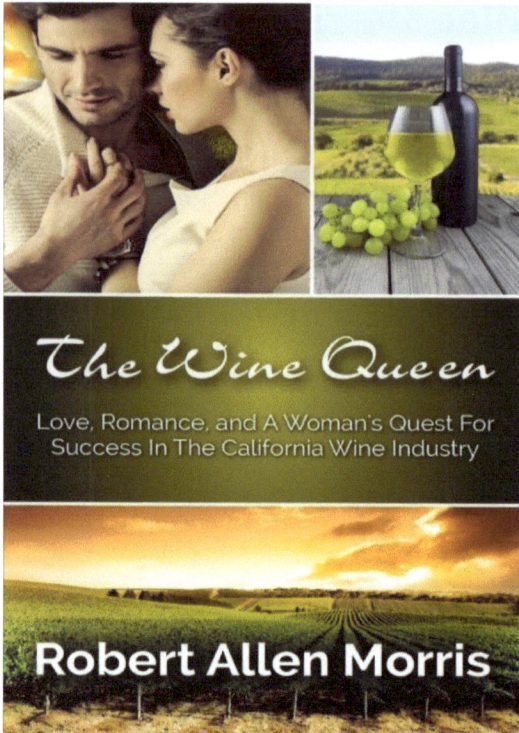

Ann Robinson is orphaned at the age of eight and sent to live with her Uncle Dave and mean-spirited, manipulative Aunt Harriett. Ann is smart, works hard in school, and goes to college. She graduates at the top of her class with a degree in economics, and accepts a job as a sales manager. When she sees Ray Collins presenting a paper at professional meetings, she becomes infatuated with him. But she learns that he's married with a family, although his marriage is troubled. Ann can't get Ray off of her mind, and ultimately decides that if she can't have Ray, then she'll never get married. She goes back to school, gets her master's degree, and climbs the corporate ladder at the Global Soft Drink Company. Ray's marriage finally ends, and when he and Ann go on their first date, they are powerfully attracted to each other. They subsequently fall deeply in love, have an incredibly romantic courtship, and get married. Ann is devastated when their marriage comes to an unexpected and abrupt end. She accepts a position as the chief financial officer for the Columbia Creek Winery, and moves to Napa, California. With the help of an equity investment from the Global Soft Drink Company, Ann buys the winery. She subsequently makes wines and develops new wine blends that become very popular and gain international recognition. Sales soar and she grows Columbia Creek Winery into the largest wine company in the world. But she never gives up on love and romance, as demonstrated by the surprising ending.

Reviewed by Valerie Rouse for Readers' Favorite

"The Wine Queen by Robert Allen Morris is a delightful story about a bright, educated young lady with good business acumen. It tells a tale about dedication. The main character, Ann Robinson, always committed herself to her goals and excelled. This is an admirable trait. Author Robert Morris did an excellent job developing the main character and displaying her inner strength and boldness. This feature is one which all readers should uphold. The tone is colloquial and quite easy to follow. I love the emphasis the author placed on the romance portion of the novel. This section was very intense emotionally and I was caught up in the rapture of the heated romance. I identified with Ann and felt that she deserved the attention and love being given. This indicates the creative genius of the author. I love the fact that the author chose to provide a little background on the upbringing of the main character. This allows the reader to understand her personality on a deeper level. The twist at the end was totally unexpected. It is not very realistic, but it is entertaining to read nevertheless. Overall, The Wine Queen is a good read, and I recommend it to all readers." *Readers' Favorite*

About The Author

Robert Allen Morris, a Florida native, is an agricultural economist with over thirty years of experience in Florida agribusiness. He is currently Vice-President of Sales and Marketing for Blue Lake Citrus Products, Inc., the company that produces and markets the Noble brand of high end specialty citrus juices as well as bulk citrus juices sold to other brands and retail chains. From 2007 until 2012, Allen was on the faculty of the University of Florida in the Food and Resource Economics Department. His responsibilities included both educational programs and research. Prior to that, he held managerial positions with various companies including Prudential Agricultural Investments, the largest lender to Florida agribusiness, Cutrale Citrus Juices USA, the North American subsidiary of Sucocitrico Cutrale, one of the world's largest citrus growers, processors and exporters, based in Araraquara, Brazil; Tropicana, one of the largest global citrus juice brands; The Cola Company; and A. Duda and Sons, Inc., a Florida-based family-owned company that produces and markets vegetables, cattle, and citrus with operations in Florida, Texas and California. Allen's advice on agribusiness has been sought after as a consultant by global soft drink companies, national and regional citrus juice brands, international agricultural asset management firms, commodity trading exchanges, insurance companies, banks, and citrus growers and processors. His clients have ranged from Fortune 100 companies, to family-owned businesses, located in Florida, New York, California, Mexico, Brazil, Europe, and China. Allen has been an invited speaker on agribusiness topics in Spain, England, Holland, Poland, Germany, Brazil, Mexico, and China, and throughout the U.S. He has taught case studies on agribusiness in executive education programs at the Harvard Business School, and been an invited speaker at international food policy meetings at Harvard University's Kennedy School of Government. He has published over thirty articles on Florida agribusiness in trade and professional journals. Allen currently resides with his wife, Kate, in Florida, and can be contacted at AllenMors@aol.com.